DEDICATION

This book is dedicated to everyone who has ever felt overburdened, worn out, or confined by life's responsibilities. I hope it serves as a reminder that you are not alone and that you can overcome burnout and regain the strength to survive if you have the correct resources, fortitude, and attitude.

This is for the parents, the professionals, the caretakers, and everyone else who sacrifices so much. I hope you have the room to put your health first and get the equilibrium you are due.

And to those who are pursuing recovery and development, may this book serve as a roadmap to a future full of tranquility, meaning, and vigor.

DISCLAIMER

This book's contents are meant primarily for general informational purposes and should not be interpreted as professional, psychological, or medical advice. Even though the methods and approaches covered are supported by research and professional opinions, each person's experience with stress, burnout, and mental health is different. If you are experiencing extreme stress, mental health issues, or burnout, it is crucial that you get tailored guidance from a trained healthcare practitioner.

Any liability or responsibility for any loss, injury, or unfavorable outcome resulting from the use or use of the material in this book is disclaimed by the author and publisher. Readers are urged to use their own discretion when making decisions and, as necessary, seek advice from medical or mental health specialists.

By using this book, you understand and agree that neither the publisher nor the author are liable for any consequences that may arise from utilizing the material.

CONTENTS

ACKNOWLEDGMENTS..1

CHAPTER 1..1

Comprehending the Effects of Burnout... 1

    1.1 Burnout: What Is It?...1

    1.2 The Burnout Anatomy... 3

    1.3 In the Contemporary World, Burnout.. 5

CHAPTER 2..9

Stress Science... 9

    2.1 Knowing How the Stress Reacts...9

    2.2 Causes of Contemporary Stress.. 12

    2.3 Recognizing Individual Stressors... 15

CHAPTER 3..18

Developing Emotional Resilience... 18

    3.1 Emotional Resilience: What is it?.. 18

    3.2 Building Resilience Capabilities.. 20

    3.3 Resilience Tools... 22

CHAPTER 4..26

Time Management Mastery.. 26

    4.1 The Relationship Between Stress and Time Management.................... 26

    4.2 Methods of Setting Priorities... 28

    4.3 Getting Rid of Procrastination.. 30

CHAPTER 5..34

Fostering a Harmonious Work-Life Harmony... 34

5.1 The Balance Myth...34

5.2 Establishing Limits.. 37

5.3 Planning for Rest and Recuperation.............................. 40

CHAPTER 6...44

Taking Care of Your Health to Prevent Burnout................ 44

6.1 The Connection Between Mental and Physical Health...................44

6.2 Rest and Sleep...47

6.3 Exercise and Methods of Relaxation............................. 51

CHAPTER 7...56

Social Support Systems... 56

7.1 The Significance of Connection......................................56

7.2 Establishing a Network of Support................................ 59

7.3 Putting Gratitude and Empathy into Practice................65

CHAPTER 8...70

Using Technology to Reduce Stress..70

8.1 Tools and Apps for Stress Relief.................................... 70

8.2 Handling Too Much Digital Information........................ 75

8.3 Establishing a Positive Connection with Technology.....................80

CHAPTER 9...85

Expert Techniques to Avoid Burnout...................................... 85

9.1 Workplaces That Prevent Burnout................................. 85

9.2 Standing Up for What You Want.................................... 91

9.3 Changing to a Healthier Professional Path................... 95

CHAPTER 10...100

Long-Term Methods for Maintaining Health.......................100

10.1 Establishing a Long-Term Routine... 100

10.2 Maintaining Flexibility in a Changing Environment.................. 104

10.3 An Unwavering Dedication to Self-Care.................................... 109

ABOUT THE AUTHOR...**114**

ACKNOWLEDGMENTS

Without the steadfast encouragement and support of numerous people, this book would not have been possible, and for that I am incredibly thankful.

I want to start by sincerely thanking my family and friends, whose unwavering support and faith in me have been a beacon of hope for me along this journey. Even in the most trying times, your tolerance, comprehension, and conviction in the significance of this effort kept me going.

I also want to thank the professionals, researchers, and specialists whose work served as a major source of inspiration for this book's content. Their efforts to raise awareness of these important concerns have been greatly appreciated, and their contributions to the field of stress management and burnout prevention have been priceless.

I would like to express my gratitude to my classmates, mentors, and coworkers who provided their perspectives, criticism, and encouragement during the writing process. Your knowledge and support made this book much better than I could have written it on my own.

Finally, I would like to express my gratitude to all of the readers who are interested in learning more about themselves, their wellbeing, and how to deal with the challenges of life in a resilient and balanced manner. This book is written for you, and I hope the techniques it offers will help you live a better, more satisfying life.

This book is the product of many people's efforts, and I will always be indebted to everyone who helped to make it, whether directly or indirectly. I appreciate your steadfast support.

CHAPTER 1

COMPREHENDING THE EFFECTS OF BURNOUT

People's perceptions of work, health, and well-being are shaped by burnout, which has emerged as a defining issue of the modern period. The notion of burnout, its anatomy, and its increasing occurrence in modern society are all covered in detail in this chapter.

1.1 Burnout: What Is It?

Burnout Definition

Long-term stress exposure causes burnout, a psychological illness that manifests as emotional tiredness, alienation, and a diminished sense of success. Burnout, a term coined in the 1970s by psychologist Herbert Freudenberger, is frequently linked to job stress but affects other facets of life, including relationships with family and friends.

Historical Background and the Development of

Burnout as a Worldwide Problem

At first, burnout was thought to be a problem exclusive to high-pressure occupations like teaching and nursing. Nonetheless, societal changes brought about by globalization, technological advancements, and the emergence of the "hustle culture" in the late 20th and early 21st centuries have made burnout a common occurrence. Burnout was formally acknowledged as an "occupational phenomenon" by the World Health Organization (WHO) in 2019, highlighting its worldwide significance.

How to Tell Burnout from Normal Stress

Burnout must be distinguished from normal stress, which is a normal reaction to difficult circumstances. Burnout is chronic and incapacitating, whereas stress can be brief and controllable. Important differences include:

- Stress causes over-engagement, elevated emotions, and a sense of urgency.
- Apathy, numbness, and disengagement are the outcomes of burnout.

Effective intervention and prevention depend on an

understanding of this distinction.

1.2 The Burnout Anatomy

The Three Burnout Dimensions

Three interrelated dimensions describe burnout:

1. Emotional Exhaustion:
- Constant weariness and a feeling of emotional depletion.
- It frequently shows up as physical symptoms like headaches or insomnia, as well as anger and trouble focusing.

2. Depersonalization:
- A feeling of disinterest or pessimism over one's job or environment.
- can result in the dehumanization of others, especially in occupations like nursing or teaching that need close communication with people.

3. Decreased Personal Accomplishment:
- A widespread feeling of failure or inefficiency.

- People's sense of self-worth is undermined when they believe their contributions are unimportant.

If these factors are not addressed right away, they combine to produce a cumulative impact that makes recovery more difficult.

The Impact of Burnout on Mental and Physical Health

The effects of burnout are not limited to mental health; they can affect physical health. Typical consequences include:

- **Mental Health:** Enhanced susceptibility to substance misuse, anxiety disorders, and depression.
- **Physical Health:** Immune system weakness, cardiovascular problems, gastrointestinal disorders, and chronic weariness.

Physical and emotional symptoms frequently interact to produce a vicious cycle in which burnout is made worse by declining health.

Prolonged Effects on Relationships and Careers

Burnout can have long-lasting effects if it is ignored:

- **Career Implications:** an increased chance of job turnover, frequent absence, and decreased productivity.
- Isolation can result from emotional retreat and irritation, which can affect both personal and professional relationships.

In extreme situations, burnout can force people to quit their jobs or need protracted recuperation.

1.3 In the Contemporary World, Burnout

Elements That Lead to Higher Burnout Rates

The contemporary society has particular difficulties that increase the likelihood of burnout:

- The "always-on" mentality that is powered by cellphones and remote work makes it difficult to distinguish between work and personal life.
- There is an unavoidable sense of demand brought on by constant notifications and email overload.

- Chronic stress is exacerbated by the work culture's emphasis on performance metrics, long workdays, and diminished job security.
- Feelings of estrangement are made worse by employers' lack of acknowledgment and assistance.

Social Expectations:
- Social media reinforces irrational expectations for productivity and success.
- The need to strike a "work-life balance" frequently turns into an additional cause of stress.

Identifying Symptoms and Indications in Both Yourself and Others

Effective intervention depends on early detection. Watch out for the following symptoms:

- A sensation of separation, anger, and chronic weariness are examples of emotional symptoms.
- Increased procrastination, disengagement from obligations, and deteriorating performance are examples of behavioral symptoms.
- Physical symptoms include recurrent headaches,

tense muscles, and stomach issues.

Promoting candid conversations about mental health in communities and at work can aid in identifying and assisting those who are burnt out.

Evidence of Burnout in Various Professions

Take into consideration the following instances to demonstrate the pervasive effects of burnout:

- **Healthcare Workers:** Many medical professionals experienced significant burnout as a result of long hours, heavy patient loads, and emotional strain, which was brought to light by the COVID-19 epidemic.
- **Educators:** High teacher burnout rates are a result of growing administrative demands, big class sizes, and a lack of resources.
- **Corporate Employees:** Software developers and engineers frequently experience burnout due to the rigorous atmosphere of the tech industry, which is marked by competitiveness and tight deadlines.

These incidents highlight the necessity of structural adjustments to address the underlying causes of burnout across a range of industries.

Going Ahead

Addressing the widespread impacts of burnout begins with a comprehensive understanding of the phenomenon. People and organizations can lessen its effects by being aware of its dimensions, health consequences, and contemporary causes. Prevention, healing, and resilience-building techniques will be examined in the upcoming chapters, providing workable answers to this difficult problem.

CHAPTER 2

STRESS SCIENCE

Human existence is inherently characterized by stress, which can lead to both positive and bad reactions. People can effectively manage stress and avoid long-term effects by being aware of the complex factors underlying it. The science of stress is thoroughly examined in this chapter, with particular attention paid to the physiological and psychological reactions, contemporary life triggers, and techniques for determining one's own stressors.

2.1 Knowing How the Stress Reacts

The Impact of Stress on the Brain and Body
A series of physiological and psychological reactions are set off by stress and are intended to safeguard and prime the body for difficulties. The fight-or-flight reaction is triggered when the hypothalamus in the brain triggers the sympathetic nervous system in response to a perceived

threat. Important procedures consist of:

- **Neurological Alterations:** The hypothalamus releases stress hormones in response to signals from the amygdala, which is responsible for processing emotions. This raises heart rate, improves concentration, and reroutes energy to essential organs.
- **Physical Reactions:** In order to prepare the body for action, stress causes the pupils to dilate, the breathing rate to increase, and the blood flow to be diverted from non-essential functions like digestion to muscles.

Although these reactions are vital in an emergency, they might have negative consequences if they are activated over an extended period of time:

- Prolonged stress response activation can damage the hippocampus, which can impact learning and memory.
- Anxiety disorders, sadness, and sleep difficulties may all be exacerbated by elevated stress hormone

levels.

Stress: Acute versus Chronic

There is a continuum of stress, and how long and how intense it lasts determines how it affects people:

- **Acute Stress:** Situational and transient, as anxiety before a presentation. Once the stressor is eliminated, acute stress usually goes away and may even be advantageous, improving performance and concentration.
- **Chronic Stress:** Persistent and long-lasting, resulting from recurring circumstances such as toxic work settings or financial challenges. Prolonged stress interferes with the body's normal healing processes and raises the risk of conditions including diabetes, heart disease, and immunological suppression.

Knowing this difference enables people to prioritize therapeutic techniques and assess their stress levels.

The Stress Cycle and Cortisol's Role

The adrenal glands release the steroid hormone cortisol, which is essential to the body's stress response:

- **Immediate Role:** During times of stress, cortisol keeps the body's glucose supply constant, boosting energy and alertness.
- Long-Term Consequences: Long-term cortisol release interferes with regular bodily processes, which can result in weight gain, especially around the abdomen.
- Immune system suppression increases the body's susceptibility to infections.
- A higher chance of developing long-term illnesses like osteoporosis and hypertension.

For both mental and physical health, cortisol levels must be kept in balance.

2.2 Causes of Contemporary Stress

Individual differences in stress triggers are influenced by both internal and external factors.

Triggers from Outside

Even the most resilient people can get overwhelmed by the many external stressors that modern life presents:

- **Work Deadlines:** Occupational burnout can result from increasing workloads, strict deadlines, and performance pressure.
- **Financial Pressures:** Increasing living expenses, debt, and unstable employment are major sources of stress.
- Time and energy can be strained while juggling relationships, family, and social demands.

Every one of these elements puts different demands on people, which adds to the chronic stress that permeates modern society.

Inner Triggers

Individual views, ideas, and cognitive patterns are frequently the source of internal triggers:

- **Perfectionism:** Self-criticism and discontent can result from the unrelenting pursuit of impossible standards.

- **Fear of Failure:** Procrastination and avoidance are common responses to anxiety about failing, which exacerbates stress.
- **Imposter Syndrome:** A chronic sense of inadequacy in the face of seeming achievement can make stress worse, especially for high achievers.

It takes honesty and introspection to identify internal triggers, which paves the way for significant change.

Social Media's Effect on Stress Levels

Social media has changed the way people interact, but it has also brought up new anxieties.

- **Comparison Culture**: Social media highlight reels cultivate sentiments of inferiority and jealousy by setting up irrational expectations.
- Constant exposure to news and opinions can cause information overload, which can result in worry and decision fatigue.
- **Addictive Behaviors:** Compulsive usage that interferes with sleep and mental health might result

from the need for approval from likes and comments.

To lessen these impacts, it is essential to strike a balance between online and offline activity.

2.3 Recognizing Individual Stressors

Effective stress management requires the capacity to recognize and comprehend one's own pressures.

Useful Resources for Self-Evaluation
People can identify their stressors and track their reactions with the aid of several tools:

- **Journaling:** Recording everyday feelings and ideas on paper helps identify triggers and recurring patterns.
- The Perceived Stress Scale (PSS) is one structured assessment tool used to quantify stress levels and pinpoint contributory causes.
- **Mindfulness Practices:** Methods such as body scans and meditation improve self-awareness and

enable people to identify stress early.

These techniques enable people to manage their stress in a proactive manner.

Comprehending Stress Trends and Patterns

Deeper insights can be obtained by examining patterns after stressors have been identified:

- **Schedule:** How frequently does the stressor happen?
- **Intensity:** To what extent does it influence your feelings or actions?
- **Duration:** What is the duration of the effects?

A person might see, for instance, that stress levels rise during Monday meetings, suggesting that preparation or boundary-setting are necessary.

The Value of Early Identification

Preventing the development of chronic stress or burnout requires early stress detection. Important advantages include:

- **Timely Intervention:** Reducing health risks and promoting a speedier recovery are two benefits of early stress management.
- **Improved Resilience:** By recognizing triggers, people can better handle stressors in the future.
- **Improved Quality of Life:** Relationships, productivity, and general well-being all improve when stress levels are lower.

People may deal with life's obstacles more easily and confidently by developing awareness and engaging in proactive stress management.

Although stress is an unavoidable aspect of life, it doesn't have to control or define it. People can take charge of their reactions by comprehending the psychological and physiological effects of stress, identifying personal stressors, and detecting contemporary triggers. We will look at ways to successfully manage stress, build resilience, and design a more balanced, healthy life in the upcoming chapters.

CHAPTER 3

Developing Emotional Resilience

The foundation of mental health is emotional resilience, which enables people to confront difficulties with fortitude and flexibility. It is about developing the ability to bounce back and develop from adversity, not about repressing feelings or bearing trials in silence. This chapter explores the idea of emotional resilience, useful strategies for cultivating it, and resources to fortify this vital life ability.

3.1 Emotional Resilience: What is it?

Resilience: Definition and Advantages
The ability to adjust, bounce back, and flourish in the face of hardship, stress, or tragedy is known as emotional resilience. It entails preserving psychological stability while negotiating the unavoidable highs and lows of life.

- The ability to tackle problems calmly and

objectively improves problem-solving abilities.
- Enhances mental well-being by decreasing the probability of anxiety and depression.
- Enhances communication and emotional control, which fortifies interpersonal bonds.

Resilience is a skill that may be cultivated over time; it is not an intrinsic quality.

The Difference Between Resilience and Just "Powering Through"

Resilience is sometimes confused with tenacity or "powering through" challenges. Resilience is about overcoming setbacks, whereas perseverance is about:

- **Adaptability:** Modifying plans and goals to accommodate evolving situations.
- Emotional regulation is the ability to control feelings in a healthy way without denying or repressing them.
- **Growth:** Taking advantage of setbacks to advance both professionally and personally.

A balanced approach is made possible by resilience, which

makes sure that perseverance doesn't come at the expense of one's physical or mental health.

3.2 Building Resilience Capabilities

Resilience is a complex ability including behavioral, emotional, and mental components. It takes deliberate work and practice to build resilience.

Developing Self-Awareness and Mindfulness

Resilience is based on self-awareness and mindfulness, which enable people to comprehend and control their emotional reactions:

- **Mindfulness Techniques:** Pay attention to the here and now without passing judgment.
- To improve awareness of thoughts and feelings, practice guided meditations.
- Exercises for Self-Awareness: Journaling to pinpoint emotional patterns and triggers.
- Frequent introspection to evaluate how one reacts to stress.

People can respond to difficulties more carefully and less reactively by developing an awareness of their inner world.

Building Optimism and Self-Efficacy
One essential element of resilience is self-efficacy, or the conviction that one can affect results:

Building Self-Efficacy:
- To gradually increase confidence, set attainable goals.
- Think back on prior accomplishments to strengthen your faith in your own talents.

Building Optimism:
- Reframe obstacles as chances for development and education.
- To turn your attention to the good things in life, cultivate thankfulness.

Even in the face of hardship, optimism fosters a hopeful view, which strengthens resilience.

Developing a Growth Mentality
Resilience requires a growth mentality, which holds that

skills may be acquired via work:

Key Principles:
- View obstacles as chances for development rather than dangers.
- Consider failure to be a normal aspect of learning.

Doable Steps:
- Ask for and make good use of feedback.
- Instead of celebrating perfection, celebrate progress.

With each experience, a growth mindset strengthens resilience by turning setbacks into learning opportunities.

3.3 Resilience Tools

Resilience strategies enable people to reinterpret negative events, manage stress, and ask for help when they need it.

Behavioral-Cognitive Strategies to Reframe Negative Thoughts

Research supports the use of cognitive-behavioral treatments (CBTs) to change harmful thought habits.

- **Identifying Cognitive Distortions:** Identify typical distortions like black-and-white thinking or catastrophizing.
- **Challenging Negative Thoughts:** Cast doubt on the veracity of pessimistic presumptions and swap them out for fair viewpoints.
- **Positive Affirmations:** To combat self-doubt and boost confidence, use encouraging statements.

Cognitive behavioral therapy (CBT) helps people escape negative thought patterns and develop a more resilient outlook.

Breathing Techniques and Meditation

Breathing techniques and meditation are effective methods for reducing stress and building emotional resilience:

- Benefits of meditation include increased focus, decreased anxiety, and improved emotional equilibrium.
- Inhale for four counts, hold for four counts, exhale for four counts, and pause for four counts. This is known as box breathing.

- **Diaphragmatic Breathing:** To trigger the body's relaxation response, deepen your breathing from the diaphragm.

By calming the nervous system, these techniques help people respond to difficulties with more composure.

Looking for Assistance Through Peer Networks and Counseling

Being resilient is not just a personal goal; social ties frequently help to reinforce it:

Counseling and Therapy:
- Offer a secure environment for examining feelings and creating coping mechanisms.
- Provide advice on how to handle difficult social or professional situations.

Peer Networks:
- Encourage a feeling of community and mutual comprehension.
- In times of adversity, offer emotional support and helpful guidance.

Creating a network of support guarantees that people are not traveling alone in their quest for resilience.

A dynamic and essential trait, emotional resilience empowers people to face life's obstacles with fortitude and flexibility. Anyone can improve their resilience by learning what resilience means, cultivating fundamental abilities like optimism and mindfulness, and using useful resources like social support and cognitive-behavioral strategies. The capacity to bounce back, develop, and prosper becomes not only a personal advantage but also a fundamental component of general well-being when life continues to bring challenges.

CHAPTER 4

TIME MANAGEMENT MASTERY

Success on both a personal and professional level depends on efficient time management. In addition to increasing productivity, it also promotes control, lowers stress levels, and avoids burnout. This chapter examines the close relationship between stress and time management, as well as useful methods for setting priorities and overcoming procrastination.

4.1 The Relationship Between Stress and Time Management

How Burnout Is Caused by Ineffective Time Management

Ineffective time management sets off a chain reaction that finally results in burnout, tension, and worry. When tasks accumulate without a clear goal or framework, people go through:

- Decision weariness can result from a lack of priority, which makes everything seem vital.
- The constant switching of attention between tasks lowers overall productivity.
- Deadlines Missed: Remorse, annoyance, and strained work relationships can result from missing deadlines.

Chronic stress brought on by balancing too many obligations without a clear plan on how to carry them out is frequently the root cause of burnout.

The Advantages of Planning for the Mind

Planning provides clarity and a sense of control, both of which are critical for lowering stress:

- **Clarity:** By dividing work into smaller, more manageable segments, ambiguity is decreased and enormous undertakings become less daunting.
- **Confidence:** Having a well-planned timetable increases one's confidence in their capacity to complete commitments and meet deadlines.

- A better work-life balance is promoted by planning, which guarantees time is set aside for both professional and personal demands.

Proactive time management helps people reduce stress and increase their capacity to deal with difficulties.

4.2 Methods of Setting Priorities

The foundation of time management is setting and achieving priorities. Knowing what to focus on first is essential when there are several obligations vying for your attention.

Eisenhower's Matrix: Important vs. Urgent Tasks

Four quadrants are used by the Eisenhower Matrix to classify tasks:

1. **Urgent and Important:** Activities that must be completed right away, such fulfilling deadlines or responding to emergencies.
2. **Important but Not Urgent:** Activities that support long-term objectives, such as skill development or

strategy planning.

3. **Urgent but Not Important:** Activities that are frequently assignable, such regular emails or small disruptions.
4. **Not Urgent and Not Important:** Time-wasting diversions, such overusing social media.

Application Tips:
- to concentrate on making significant progress, dedicate the majority of your time on Quadrant 2 tasks.
- Reduce the distractions in Quadrant 4 to recover time.
- Tasks in Quadrant 3 should be assigned whenever feasible.

Techniques for Pomodoro and Time-Blocking

Time-blocking and the Pomodoro Technique are two efficient ways to organize your day:

- **Time-Blocking:** Set aside specified time blocks for tasks or groups of tasks, including meetings, concentrated work, or leisure. This approach

guarantees that each priority has a specific time slot.
- The Pomodoro Technique involves working in concentrated bursts of time, usually lasting 25 minutes, and then taking a little break.
- Benefits include increased concentration, less exhaustion, and a distinct sensation of achievement.

Determining Reasonable Expectations and Goals

Setting unrealistic goals can cause dissatisfaction and lower motivation. To establish attainable objectives:

Divide more complex jobs into manageable, smaller tasks.

- Employ SMART (Specific, Measurable, Achievable, Relevant, Time-bound) as your framework.
- To keep plans in line with your goals, evaluate progress on a regular basis and make any adjustments.

4.3 Getting Rid of Procrastination

One of the main barriers to efficient time management is procrastination. To overcome it, you must comprehend its underlying causes.

Psychological Factors and Habits That Contribute to Procrastination

Psychological variables like the following frequently cause procrastination:

- **Fear of Failure:** Avoidance of tasks because of fear of performing poorly.
- **Perfectionism:** Postponing action due to irrational demands for faultless performance.
- Lack of motivation is the inability to recognize the immediate benefit or reward of doing an activity.

Short-term gratification can also fuel procrastination, as in the case of social media browsing rather than taking on a difficult task.

Suggestions for Overcoming Procrastination and Maintaining Motivation

Intentional strategies are necessary to break the pattern of procrastination:

- To overcome inertia, start with a tiny, manageable portion of a task.
- **Establish Clear Deadlines:** Self-imposed deadlines foster accountability and a sense of urgency.
- **Reward Progress:** To keep yourself motivated and optimistic, acknowledge and celebrate your accomplishments.

Using Technology and Tools to Improve Time Management

There are several methods available in modern technology to improve time management and fight procrastination:

- **Task Management Apps:** Programs such as Microsoft To-Do, Asana, or Trello facilitate task organization and progress monitoring.
- **Focus Apps:** Programs like Forest or Focus@Will reduce distractions by encouraging focus.
- The integration of digital calendars with reminders guarantees that nothing is overlooked.

Productivity may be increased and procrastination effectively controlled by fusing useful techniques with technology.

Developing a balanced and satisfying life is the goal of time management skills, not just doing duties. People may take charge of their schedules and confidently accomplish their goals by comprehending the connection between stress and time management, implementing tried-and-true prioritization strategies, and confronting procrastination. With deliberate and strategic management, time, a limited resource, turns into an ally rather than an enemy.

CHAPTER 5

FOSTERING A HARMONIOUS WORK-LIFE HARMONY

One of the most sought-after objectives in the fast-paced world of today is striking a healthy work-life balance. It can be very stressful to constantly balance work and personal obligations. Although it may appear desirable to have a perfect balance, balance is actually a dynamic, ever-evolving concept. It calls for awareness, adaptation, and deliberate effort. This chapter explores how to establish boundaries, prioritize relaxation and recuperation, and comprehend the subtleties of a healthy work-life balance.

5.1 The Balance Myth

Recognizing That Everyone's Definition of Balance Is Different

The idea of work-life balance is quite personal and differs from person to person. Some people may define balance as being able to work from home, while others may define it as having enough time for hobbies, family, or personal growth. To achieve this equilibrium, there is no one-size-fits-all formula. The important thing is to understand that what is considered "balance" varies depending on personal needs, objectives, and situations.

- A working parent may have a different definition of balance than someone without children or family obligations.
- **Career Stage:** While someone approaching retirement may choose more personal time, a young professional may emphasize career advancement.
- **Health and Well-Being:** People who are dealing with health issues may put their desire for relaxation and recuperation ahead of their professional goals.

Determine what balance means to you rather than striving for a universally unattainable ideal. What are my values, you ask? What career goals do I have in mind? What fulfills me when I'm not working? Setting these priorities makes it simpler to allocate your time and effort appropriately.

Determining Individual Priorities and Values

Knowing what is most important to you is the first step towards creating a healthy work-life balance. How you spend your time and energy is influenced by your values.

- **Family and Relationships:** Maintaining close personal ties with family and friends is a major concern for some people.
- **Personal Development and Hobbies**: Other people could value lifelong learning or making time for personal interests.
- **Professional Objectives:** Some people could be career-driven and consider their accomplishments in the workplace to be essential to their value as persons.

Take into consideration the following actions to gain clarity about your values:

- **Reflect:** Consider what makes you feel fulfilled on a regular basis.
- Set priorities by prioritizing your values and

modifying your time commitments accordingly.
- **Examine and modify:** Your values are dynamic, just like life itself. Periodically reevaluate to make sure your balance still meets your changing needs.

5.2 Establishing Limits

Saying "no" to unnecessary commitments is crucial.
Being able to say "no" is one of the most effective strategies for preserving work-life balance. It can be difficult to decline more obligations in a culture that frequently promotes busyness. Saying "yes" to everything, though, can rapidly result in stress, fatigue, and resentment.

Setting boundaries entails identifying your limits and knowing when you are being overextended. This can be accomplished by:

- **Clear Communication:** You can set expectations and avoid overcommitment by politely but clearly explaining your availability and limits.
- **Assessment of Requests:** Consider how well a task fits with your present priorities and values before

accepting it. Does it help you achieve your personal or professional objectives?

- **Preventing Guilt:** Saying no guarantees that you are protecting your wellbeing and that you will be able to perform effectively when it really counts, which does not imply that you are careless or self-centered.

Using Clear Communication to Manage Work Expectations

Managing job expectations and guaranteeing a manageable workload need effective communication with coworkers, bosses, and clients. Saying no is only one aspect of setting boundaries; another is being proactive in identifying what you can and cannot do.

- **Explain Your Boundaries:** Openly discuss your bandwidth with your management or team if you are overworked.
- **Establish Expectations:** Indicate whether any projects will affect your work-life balance or whether some tasks will take longer than expected.
- **Request Assistance:** When necessary, don't be afraid to assign chores or seek assistance. The secret

to keeping a sustainable workload is teamwork.

Recommendations for Disconnecting from Work After Hours

Disconnecting from work after hours is one of the biggest obstacles to preserving a positive work-life balance. The urge to be "always on," checking emails and responding to communications outside of work hours, is something that many people experience. To unplug successfully:

Establish distinct start and end times for your workday by setting certain work hours. Make a conscious effort to turn off your computer or leave your desk at the end of the workday.

- **Technological Mindfulness:** To prevent continual disruptions, turn off email alerts after business hours. To establish a work-free zone, use features like "Do Not Disturb" on your phone.
- Establish a Ritual: Create a routine, like going for a walk or doing something fun, to mark the end of your workday. This facilitates the mental transition from work to leisure time.

5.3 Planning for Rest and Recuperation

Vacations and Mental Health Days: Their Significance

For long-term productivity, creativity, and mental health, taking time off from work is crucial. To avoid burnout and improve general well being, regular vacations and mental health days are essential.

- **Vacations:** Taking a break from the routine enables rest, discovery, and renewal. People who take regular holidays report feeling less stressed and more satisfied with their jobs, according to studies.
- **Days for Mental Health:** Taking a day off to prioritize mental health can occasionally be just as crucial as going on vacation. People can recharge and avoid emotional tiredness by taking mental health days as necessary.

It's critical to consider vacation time as an investment in your long-term productivity and well-being rather than as a luxury. Instead of waiting until you are overburdened, make sure to plan these pauses.

Including Relaxation Techniques Every Day

Daily relaxation techniques, in addition to trips and days dedicated to mental health, can have a big impact on leading a balanced life. These techniques support better mental health and stress management:

- **Meditation and Mindfulness:** By calming the mind, mindfulness practice lowers anxiety and keeps you in the moment. Stress levels can be decreased by using methods like deep breathing exercises or meditation, which trigger the body's relaxation response.
- **Physical Exercise:** Frequent exercise promotes both physical and emotional well-being and is a potent stress reducer. Stretching activities or even a quick daily walk can improve mood and energy levels.
- **Passions and Recreation:** A vital way to unwind is to partake in enjoyable pursuits like cooking, drawing, or reading. Outside of work, these pursuits offer a platform for relaxation and artistic expression.

Spotting the Indications That You Need a Break

Maintaining a healthy work-life balance requires knowing when you need to take a break. Burnout results from people frequently ignoring early warning indicators of stress and exhaustion. Important signs that it might be time to take a break include:

- **Physical Symptoms:** Headaches, exhaustion, and tense muscles may indicate a need for rest.
- **Emotional Exhaustion:** Disconnecting and recharging is necessary if you feel emotionally spent, aloof, or irritated all the time.
- **Reduction in Productivity:** It can be a sign that you are overworking yourself if your performance is suffering even if you are putting in more hours.

You can take proactive measures to rest and recuperate before burnout sets in by recognizing these symptoms early.

Maintaining a healthy work-life balance is a continuous process that calls for mindfulness, self-awareness, and deliberate effort. It's critical to understand that everyone will have a different optimum balance. This balance requires practicing relaxing, prioritizing rest, and establishing clear boundaries. You may design a life that combines career success and personal joy by knowing your values, making time for healing, and skillfully managing expectations. Finding equilibrium that enables you to succeed in both areas is more important than striving for perfection when it comes to work and life balance.

CHAPTER 6

Taking Care of Your Health to Prevent Burnout

In order to prevent burnout and preserve a positive work-life balance, physical wellness is essential. The mind is better able to manage stress, process emotions, and sustain high performance levels when the body is in peak condition. This chapter explores the deep relationship between mental and physical health, the value of sleep and recuperation, and how to incorporate relaxation and physical activity into everyday life.

6.1 The Connection Between Mental and Physical Health

How Exercise Improves Mood and Reduces Stress

One of the best strategies for overcoming burnout is exercise. It has a substantial positive impact on mental health in addition to physical health. Frequent exercise causes the body's natural mood enhancers, endorphins, to be released, which lowers stress and elevates mood. By interacting with the brain's receptors, endorphins function as natural antidepressants, fostering feelings of wellbeing and euphoria.

- **Reduction of Stress:** Exercise lowers the body's cortisol levels. Stress causes the release of the hormone cortisol, which can cause medical conditions like hypertension as well as mental health issues like anxiety and depression. By controlling the synthesis of cortisol, physical activity helps to lessen this.
- **Elevated Emotion:** Exercise, especially aerobic activities like swimming, cycling, or running, improves blood flow to the brain, which can improve mood and cognitive function.
- **Cognition of the Mind:** It has been demonstrated that regular exercise enhances memory, cognitive function, and mental clarity in general. By increasing blood flow to the brain, exercise promotes improved cognitive function by supplying the brain with more oxygen and nutrients. As a result, one can concentrate better, think more clearly under pressure,

and experience less brain fog.

Incorporating exercise into daily routines helps those who are burnt out by promoting physical health and offering a much-needed mental reset that boosts emotional resilience and energy levels.

Nutrition's Impact on Energy and Mental Clarity

A healthy diet is essential for preserving both physical and emotional well-being. Our feelings, thoughts, and actions throughout the day are directly influenced by the food we consume. Positive mood, long-lasting energy, and mental clarity can all be greatly enhanced by eating a balanced diet.

- **Brain-Boosting Foods:** Omega-3 fatty acids, which are present in foods like nuts, seeds, and fish, are among the nutrients that are known to promote brain health. Maintaining cognitive function and lowering the danger of mental weariness require these good fats.
- **Complex Carbohydrates to Provide Consistent Energy:** Complex carbs, which are found in whole

grains, fruits, and vegetables, release energy gradually, preserving stable blood sugar levels and avoiding the energy spikes that accompany sugary foods.

- **Hydration:** Dehydration can affect mood and cognitive function, making it more difficult to concentrate and think effectively. Maintaining proper hydration helps avoid weariness, which can worsen stress, and preserve mental clarity.

- **The Influence of Micronutrients:** The neurological system depends on vitamins and minerals like folate, vitamin B12, and magnesium. Burnout may worsen as a result of symptoms like exhaustion, worry, and irritability brought on by a lack of essential nutrients.

Our dietary decisions have the power to either increase or decrease our energy levels. We can sustain our mental health, stay focused, and have the energy we need to fight burnout by making nutrient-dense food choices.

6.2 Rest and Sleep

Recognizing the Value of Restful Sleep

Sleep is essential for both physical and mental well-being. It is essential for immune system function, emotional control, cognitive function, and general recuperation. Burnout is directly caused by inadequate or poor-quality sleep, which makes it harder to handle stress and causes both physical and emotional tiredness.

- **Brain Function and Sleep:** The brain processes emotions, organizes memories, and gets rid of garbage when we sleep. While sleep deprivation results in decreased cognitive function, mood swings, and increased stress, adequate sleep enhances decision-making, problem-solving, and memory recall.
- **Emotional Regulation and Sleep:** Sleep has an impact on how emotions are controlled. Lack of sleep causes the brain's emotional regions, including the amygdala, to become more reactive, which can result in irritation, anxiety, and inadequate coping skills.
- **Sleep and Physical Recuperation:** The body also physically repairs and restores itself as we sleep. Deep sleep causes the release of growth hormone,

which supports immunological and muscular regeneration. These functions are hampered by sleep deprivation, making the body more susceptible to disease and physical exhaustion.

Resilience is largely dependent on getting enough good sleep. It restores energy stores and enables the body to recuperate from everyday pressures, both of which are necessary for sustained productivity and mental clarity.

Suggestions to Enhance Sleep Quality
Adopting appropriate sleep hygiene routines is crucial to enhancing the quality of your sleep. These behaviors facilitate the body's transition into deeper, more restorative sleep stages and help to establish an atmosphere that supports sound sleep.

Maintaining a regular sleep schedule, including on weekends, makes it easier for the body to fall asleep and wake up naturally. This is achieved by going to bed and waking up at the same time each day.

- **Restrict Stimulants:** Steer clear of smoking, coffee, and large meals right before bed because these substances can disrupt the body's natural capacity to unwind and go to sleep.

- **Establish a Calm Bedtime Routine:** You may tell your body it's time to settle down by doing soothing things like reading, having a warm bath, or meditating.

- **Optimize Your Sleep Environment:** Create a calm and cozy sleeping environment in your bedroom. This includes lowering noise levels, minimizing screen time before bed, and making sure the space is cool and dark.

Aware of the Risks Associated with Lack of Sleep

Lack of sleep can have detrimental effects on one's physical and emotional well-being. Chronic sleep deprivation raises the risk of heart disease, diabetes, and obesity, among other illnesses. In terms of the mind, it might result in emotional instability, poor judgment, and memory loss.

- **Mood Impact:** Lack of sleep impairs the brain's capacity to control emotions, which increases stress, worry, and despair.

- **Reduced Productivity and Cognitive Function:** Sleep deprivation can affect one's ability to concentrate, pay attention, and solve problems, which makes it challenging to carry out everyday duties efficiently.
- **Weakened Immune System:** Prolonged sleep deprivation impairs immunity, increasing susceptibility to disease and lengthening recovery periods.

In order to prevent burnout and preserve general wellbeing, it is essential to acknowledge the significance of sleep and take action to enhance its quality.

6.3 Exercise and Methods of Relaxation

Including Exercise in a Busy Schedule

It's not necessary to spend hours at the gym to be physically active. It's critical for those with hectic schedules to figure out how to fit movement into their everyday activities. Frequent exercise improves mood, increases energy, and lowers stress, all of which can help fight burnout.

- A mental reset and a reduction in burnout can be achieved by taking regular walks throughout the day, whether they be brisk walks at lunch breaks or walking meetings.
- **Stretching and Desk Exercises:** Stretching and basic desk exercises can help reduce muscle tension and increase circulation for people who work in sedentary conditions.
- **Active Commuting**: If at all possible, riding a bike or walking to work can be a terrific way to include exercise into your day and lower your stress levels.

It is crucial to include movement in everyday routines, not only for physical health but also as a potent strategy to fight mental exhaustion and burnout.

Tai Chi, Yoga, and Other Stress-Reduction Activities
Stress reduction and relaxation are greatly enhanced by mindful movement practices such as yoga, tai chi, and others. These exercises can reduce cortisol levels, improve flexibility, and foster mental clarity by combining physical postures with mindfulness and controlled breathing.

- **Yoga:** By encouraging profound relaxation and mental clarity, yoga has been demonstrated to lower stress and anxiety. Certain techniques, such vinyasa or restorative yoga, can aid in easing mental and physical stress.
- **Tai Chi:** Tai Chi, a low-impact workout that emphasizes slow, deliberate movements, is well-known for enhancing mental clarity, flexibility, and balance. Its contemplative elements promote serenity and lessen tension.
- **Mentality in Motion:** By concentrating on movement and breathing to relieve stress, these exercises help people establish a connection with their bodies. Emotional resilience can be greatly increased by integrating mindfulness with physical exercise.

The Science Underpinning Progressive Muscle Relaxation and Other Relaxation Techniques

The relaxation method known as progressive muscle relaxation (PMR) entails tensing and then relaxing various bodily muscle groups. By raising awareness of physical tension and letting the body release it, this technique has been shown to help lower stress and encourage relaxation.

- **How PMR Works:** PMR trains people to identify and deliberately release regions of stress by methodically tensing and relaxing muscle groups.
- **Stress Reduction:** By stimulating the parasympathetic nervous system, PMR lowers blood pressure, slows the heartbeat, and fosters relaxation.
- It has been demonstrated that PMR enhances the quality of sleep by promoting relaxation in the body before bedtime.

In the battle against burnout, relaxation methods like PMR are crucial since they encourage both mental and bodily calm.

Maintaining general well-being and preventing burnout require fostering physical health. In order to lower stress and promote resilience, it is essential to use relaxation techniques, eat a healthy diet, get enough sleep, and exercise. People can avoid burnout, increase mental clarity, and improve their emotional well-being by incorporating these behaviors into their daily lives. The basis of a balanced, satisfying life is a healthy body, which in turn promotes a healthy mind.

CHAPTER 7

Social Support Systems

When it comes to mental health and avoiding burnout, the importance of social ties cannot be overstated. Since humans are social creatures, our relationships—both personal and professional—form the basis of our ability to withstand stress. This chapter examines the significant contribution that social support networks make to reducing burnout, how to create and fortify your support system, and the value of empathy and thankfulness in fostering these connections.

7.1 The Significance of Connection

Relationships' Contribution to Stress Reduction

Stress levels and general mental health have been demonstrated to be directly and significantly impacted by human connection. Relationships whether with friends, family, or coworkers serve as a protective barrier against the damaging impacts of stress. Strong support networks, which provide both practical and emotional assistance, help people deal with life's obstacles more skillfully.

- **Emotional Support:** Emotional support is one of the most crucial elements of relationships. Anxiety, loneliness, and tension can be reduced by having someone to talk to who listens, understands, and provides consolation. Strong emotional support networks help people bounce back from stressful situations faster and are more resilient in the face of adversity, according to studies.
- **Pragmatic Support**: Support systems also offer practical assistance. Practical support, whether it be in the form of help with daily duties or counsel and direction during trying moments, can lessen the mental strain and help avoid burnout.
- **Sense of Belonging:** A sense of belonging is fostered by social connections and is crucial for mental health. You feel more purposeful and emotionally secure when you know that you belong to a community, whether it be your family, friends, or professional network.

A foundation of stability and reassurance is provided by having supportive, caring connections, which can lessen stress and enhance general wellbeing.

The Impact of Isolation on Burnout Symptoms

Conversely, isolation has a negative effect on mental health. When people are lonely, the lack of emotional support or social engagement can make burnout, stress, and anxiety symptoms worse. People who are alone miss out on opportunities to express their emotions, get guidance, and get emotional support all of which are critical for stress management.

- **Insufficient Emotional Release:** Emotional tiredness can result from feelings of irritation, despair, and overload that accumulate when there is no one to talk to. Emotional repression can exacerbate feelings of loneliness and make stress management more difficult.
- **Impact on cognition:** Cognitive function can be hampered by loneliness. According to studies, extended periods of isolation can have a detrimental

impact on memory, judgment, and problem-solving skills—all of which are essential for handling stress at work and in daily life.

- **Potential Health Consequences:** Chronic loneliness is associated with a higher risk of mental health conditions like anxiety and depression as well as physical health problems like high blood pressure and heart disease.

- **Maintaining Pessimistic Thoughts:** Negative mental patterns can also be sustained by isolation. When people are alone themselves, they could obsess over their problems, which might exacerbate their anxieties and lead to burnout.

To put it briefly, loneliness creates a vicious cycle of tension and exhaustion that gets harder to escape. On the other hand, social support acts as a buffer, giving people the resources they need to deal with and get past these obstacles.

7.2 Establishing a Network of Support

Fortifying Current Connections

Developing your current relationships is the first step in creating a robust social support system. These current relationships, whether with friends, family, or coworkers, can serve as the foundation of your support network. It takes deliberate effort, open communication, and vulnerability to strengthen these ties.

- **The key is communication:** Strong relationships are built on effective communication. Deeper emotional connections are fostered when you take the time to actively listen to people and freely express your feelings. People are more inclined to help when you need it when they feel acknowledged and understood.
- **Consistent Check-Ins:** You may keep your connections strong by checking in with your loved ones on a regular basis. It demonstrates your concern for their welfare and your availability for them in times of need. This reciprocal assistance fosters emotional stability and trust, which makes it simpler to lean on them in trying situations.
- **Establishing Boundaries:** Mutual respect and understanding are the cornerstones of healthy

relationships. Relationship balance depends on both parties setting and upholding boundaries. People are more inclined to provide sincere assistance during stressful situations when they believe that their needs are being addressed and that their personal space is being respected.

- **Time Dedicated to Relationships:** Like everything else in life, relationships need time and work to succeed. Setting aside time for family and friends, even if it's just for a quick phone conversation or a quick cup of coffee, strengthens your bonds and demonstrates your appreciation for them.

You may build a strong support system that can assist you in managing stress and avoiding burnout by making investments in the relationships that are most important to you.

Being a part of communities and support groups

You can greatly improve your well-being by looking for new sources of support in addition to fortifying current ones. A sense of community and the opportunity to exchange experiences with those facing comparable difficulties can be gained by joining support groups or communities.

- **Assist Teams for Common Experiences:** Making connections with people who are going through similar things gives many people comfort. Shared experiences can offer validation and a sense of solidarity, whether it's in a community for a specific activity or interest, a stress-reduction club related to the workplace, or a mental health support group.
- **Internet Communities:** Online communities provide a forum for people to interact, exchange guidance, and provide support in the current digital era. You have the chance to broaden your support network through social media groups, forums, and online peer support networks, especially for people who might feel alone because of social or geographic constraints.
- **Networks for Professionals:** Participating in industry or professional groups can be a great way to get support at work. In addition to encouraging information exchange and career advancement, these communities provide chances to form deep

professional connections that can provide support and direction in trying times.

- **Altruism with Volunteering:** Additionally, volunteering or taking part in charitable endeavors provides a feeling of purpose and community. In order to fight burnout, helping others can foster a sense of fulfillment and belonging.

Creating a varied support system by interacting with different groups via social, professional, or personal channels guarantees that you have a number of people to turn to for assistance when you need it.

Seeking Expert Assistance When Required

In certain situations, community support and interpersonal interactions might not be sufficient to adequately treat stress, burnout, or mental health concerns. In these situations, getting expert help can be an essential part of the healing process.

- **Counselors and Therapists:** Support from a professional mental health provider offers a secure environment for people to examine their emotions, acquire new perspectives, and create coping mechanisms. Counselors and therapists are educated to help people deal with challenging emotions and offer research-backed strategies to lessen stress and control burnout.

- **The mentors and coaches:** Life coaches or mentors can provide assistance in areas such as goal-setting, personal development, and job advancement in addition to therapy. They offer direction and responsibility, assisting people in staying on course when dealing with burnout or difficult circumstances.
- **Programs for Employee Assistance (EAPs):** EAPs, which give employees access to tools and counseling services to help them manage stress, anxiety, and other mental health issues, are available in many businesses. By making use of these services, people can get the expert assistance they require without the stigma that is frequently connected to obtaining mental health treatment.

Seeking professional assistance is a proactive measure to preserve wellbeing and stop burnout from getting worse, not a show of weakness.

7.3 Putting Gratitude and Empathy into Practice

The Benefits of Assisting Others in Reducing Personal Stress

As vital as it is to ask for help from others, it is equally necessary for mental health to assist people in return. Helping others, whether it be by lending a hand, listening, or offering emotional support, creates a sense of purpose and lowers stress levels.

- **Altruism and Mental Health:** Better mental health outcomes have been associated with helping others. Generosity and kindness can lower negative emotions like anxiety and despair, increase feelings of self-worth, and foster a sense of community.
- **Reciprocal Assistance:** Supporting others frequently results in obtaining support in return. In order to prevent burnout, social networks must be stronger and more robust, which is achieved through this reciprocal act of kindness.
- **Reduction of Stress**: Assisting others might

temporarily relieve stress by refocusing attention from one's own issues to the needs of others. People can get perspective, reduce anxiety, and cultivate happy feelings thanks to this diversion.

In addition to helping others, those who demonstrate empathy and provide support also improve their own mental health by lowering stress and fostering a more resilient mindset.

Developing Appreciation to Turn Stress Into Positivity

An effective strategy for lowering stress and enhancing mental health is gratitude. One's mindset can be significantly impacted by changing the focus from what is going wrong to what is going right.

- Regular gratitude exercises, such as writing, meditation, or just setting aside time each day to think on what you have to be grateful for, can help you reframe negative ideas and cultivate a more optimistic perspective.
- **Resilience on an emotional level:** By directing attention away from stressors, practicing

thankfulness lessens the emotional effect of trying circumstances. By developing emotional resilience, this exercise helps people deal with obstacles more effectively and recover from failures faster.

- **Fortifying Connections:** Thanking others for their help and generosity improves connections and fosters a climate of respect and concern for one another. Being grateful strengthens social ties and fosters a feeling of community by reinforcing pleasant emotions.

People can establish a positive feedback loop that helps them refocus their attention from stress and exhaustion to connection and appreciation by practicing gratitude.

Developing Support for One Another Through Active Listening

Building solid support networks and maintaining good relationships both depend on active listening. Active listening fosters an atmosphere where people feel comfortable expressing their ideas and feelings because it demonstrates empathy, understanding, and respect.

- Active listening entails paying close attention, refraining from interruptions, and refraining from making judgments. This fosters emotional health and lowers stress by providing a safe environment for people to express themselves.
- **Comprehension and Empathy:** People can demonstrate empathy and affirm others' feelings by actively listening to them. In partnerships, this reciprocal support strengthens emotional bonds and increases trust.
- The use of nonverbal communication Observing non-verbal indicators like tone of voice, body language, and facial expressions is another aspect of active listening. In addition to improving communication, this makes sure that everyone feels heard and understood.

By creating strong, trustworthy relationships and making sure that each member feels appreciated, active listening contributes to the development of a supporting network.

People can greatly lower their risk of burnout and enhance their general well-being by concentrating on creating and enhancing social support networks, exercising empathy, and developing gratitude. In addition to helping people manage stress, social ties foster a sense of community and emotional fortitude, both of which are critical for succeeding in the fast-paced, high-pressure world of today.

CHAPTER 8

Using Technology to Reduce Stress

In the fast-paced world of today, technology is a major factor in both causing and reducing stress. Digital technologies can be a source of distraction and overwhelm, but they can also offer useful methods for stress management, mindfulness training, and mental health enhancement. This chapter explores the possible advantages and disadvantages of utilizing technology to alleviate stress, provides advice on how to have a positive relationship with technology, and describes doable tactics for handling digital overload.

8.1 Tools and Apps for Stress Relief

Organization, Journaling, and Meditation Apps

Apps are among the most popular and easily available ways to use technology to reduce stress. By assisting people in maintaining organization, developing awareness, and controlling their emotions, these skills can help people feel less stressed. Apps for stress management come in a variety of forms, each with special advantages.

- **Apps for Meditation:** It has long been known that mindfulness and meditation are useful techniques for lowering stress and enhancing emotional health. People may unwind, concentrate, and clear their minds with the use of apps like Headspace, Calm, and Insight Timer, which provide breathing techniques, mindfulness exercises, and guided meditation sessions. These apps offer versatility, enabling users to choose sessions according to their need, whether they relaxation, stress reduction, or better sleep.
- **Apps for Journaling**: By giving people a platform to express their ideas and feelings and assisting them in processing challenging emotions, journaling is a tried-and-true method of stress management. With the help of apps like Day One and Journey Users can write about their everyday experiences, make plans, or think back on their ideas. Journaling's advantages for mental health can be further increased by

combining it with exercises that promote mindfulness, self-compassion, and thankfulness.

- **Apps for Productivity and Organization:** Stress can be exacerbated by a lack of structure and ineffective time management. Users may organize their tasks, establish priorities, and stay on top of duties with the use of apps like Todoist, Trello, and Evernote. These apps help people feel more in control by enhancing organization, which lessens feelings of overwhelm and makes it simpler to concentrate on one job at a time.

When it comes to cultivating mindfulness, managing everyday anxieties, and advancing mental clarity, these digital tools can be immensely beneficial. They give people useful strategies to take charge of their well-being by offering structure, relaxing activities, and time for introspection.

The Benefits and Drawbacks of Using Technology to Reduce Stress

Even while technology provides effective stress-reduction techniques, it's important to weigh the advantages and disadvantages of utilizing these apps. The way they are used determines how effective they are, just like any other instrument.

Advantages:

- **Convenience:** The accessibility of stress-relieving apps is one of its main advantages. With these tools at your fingertips, you can utilize them anywhere, at any time, whether you're at home, at work, or on the go.
- **Adjustability:** Because many applications are configurable, users can select the kind of activity or information that best meets their needs at any given time. These apps can be customized to your tastes, whether you need a brief breathing exercise or a lengthy meditation session.
- **Monitoring Progress:** A lot of stress-relieving apps have tools that let users monitor their progress, which keeps them inspired and helps them notice changes over time. Journaling apps, for instance, can monitor your mood over the course of weeks or months, giving you insight into how your mental state changes.

- **In terms of affordability:** A large audience can use these applications because many of them are free or require a cheap subscription.

The following are some drawbacks:
- **Over-Reliance on Technology:** Even while these apps can be quite beneficial, focusing too much on technology can cause a person to lose touch with their actual surroundings and themselves. The desired stress-relieving effects may be countered by excessive screen usage, which can lead to digital weariness.
- **Overwhelming Information:** Certain apps, especially those that emphasize productivity, have the potential to overwhelm users with an incessant barrage of notifications and information. Instead of reducing stress, the pressure to complete daily activities or monitor every emotion may make it worse.
- The absence of personalization Apps can offer broad advice, but they frequently don't offer the individualized, one-on-one assistance that people may require for more complex problems. To address

more complicated concerns in these situations, professional treatment or counseling may be required.

- **Privacy Issues:** Numerous apps request personal information from users, such as location, mood, and health information. Before using these apps, privacy and data security should be carefully considered, particularly if sensitive information is being exchanged.

In summary, although stress-relieving applications can be effective tools for stress management, it is important to use them carefully and sparingly to make sure they enhance rather than replace other stress-reduction techniques.

8.2 Handling Too Much Digital Information

Identifying the Times When Technology Adds to Stress
As helpful as technology can be in stress management, if it is not used carefully, it can also greatly increase feelings of overwhelm, worry, and burnout. When the never-ending stream of emails, notifications, social media posts, and work-related correspondence becomes too much to

manage, it's known as digital overload. This may cause cognitive exhaustion, impair concentration, and raise stress levels.

- **Overuse of Screen Time:** Whether for business or pleasure, spending a lot of time in front of a screen can lead to both physical and mental fatigue. Long-term screen time can increase stress by causing eye strain, irregular sleep habits, and a diminished attention span.
- **Constant Communication:** There may be an underlying sense of pressure from the expectation of always having access to emails, messages, and social media. Anxiety and difficulty focusing can result from FOMO, or the fear of missing out, and the incessant impulse to check messages.
- **Overwhelming Information:** It can be challenging to sort through the deluge of information on the internet and choose what is important, which can lead to emotions of confusion and uncertainty. Mental exhaustion brought on by the constant barrage of information, viewpoints, and assignments can make it more difficult to focus and set priorities.

The first step in managing digital overload and creating healthier tech habits is identifying when technology is making stress worse.

Methods to Reduce Electronic Distractions

It's critical to take proactive measures to reduce distractions and establish a healthier digital environment as soon as you realize that technology is causing stress. The detrimental effects of digital overload can be lessened by implementing the following tactics:

- **Assign Particular Time Slots for Technology Use**: Instead of always checking your email or phone, schedule specific times throughout the day to use technology. For instance, set aside thirty minutes each morning and afternoon to check and reply to emails, after which you should switch off your notifications for the remainder of the day.
- Turn off notifications that aren't absolutely necessary. Disabling unused alerts is one of the best strategies to reduce digital distractions. It's not necessary to be notified each time you get a new

social media post, email, or message. Restrict notifications to the most important warnings.

- **Make Use of Focus-Boosting Resources:** Apps that restrict distracting websites and promote in-depth work, such as attention@Will, Freedom, and Forest, can help you maintain attention. By reducing distractions, these apps assist users in creating a productive digital environment.

- **Plan Your Tech-Free Time:** Set aside specific times when you turn off your screens entirely. This could take place before bed, during meals, or when taking a daily stroll. Setting aside time for technology-free activities enables you to psychologically rejuvenate and re-establish a connection with the present.

You may decrease the stress that technology can occasionally generate, eliminate distractions, and reclaim control over your digital surroundings by putting these strategies into practice.

Effectively Practicing Digital Detoxes

Taking deliberate pauses from screens and technology to rest and recharge is known as a "digital detox." Unplugging from electronics on a regular basis is essential for lowering stress and improving general wellbeing.

- **Begin Small:** Start with modest, achievable objectives if you're new to digital detoxification, like setting aside an hour each day to avoid screens. As you get more accustomed to unplugging, gradually extend the duration of your disconnected time.
- **Indulge in Offline Activities:** Make use of your detox period to partake in non-technological activities like reading, working out, or going outside. Hobbies that are offline aid in reestablishing mental equilibrium and lessen the tension brought on by digital excess.
- **Create Tech-Free Areas:** Set aside some rooms of your house, such the dining room or bedroom, as tech-free zones. Without the distraction of electronic gadgets, this fosters better habits, relaxation, and interpersonal connections.
- Establish clear boundaries by informing friends, family, and coworkers about your digital detox periods so they know when you will be inaccessible. Establishing limits makes it more likely that people

will respect your desire for tech-free time.

You may rebalance your relationship with technology and escape the stress of continual connectedness with the help of a well-executed digital detox.

8.3 Establishing a Positive Connection with Technology

Maintaining a Balance Between Screen Time and Offline Activities

Even while technology is a necessary component of contemporary living, it's crucial to strike a healthy balance between screen time and offline pursuits. Including offline activities in your daily routine is crucial for preserving your general well being because prolonged screen time can cause both physical and mental exhaustion.

- **Physical Exercise:** One of the best ways to combat the negative effects of excessive screen time is to incorporate physical activity into your daily routine. Frequent exercise enhances cognitive function, lowers stress, and elevates mood.
- **Insightful pastimes:** Take part in relaxing and

mindfulness-promoting hobbies like knitting, gardening, or painting. These offline pastimes offer a chance to detach from digital distractions and give one's mind a rest.

- **Social Interaction:** In-person relationships with friends and family are crucial for mental health. Set aside time for socializing away from screens, whether it's over a meal or a stroll with a friend.

You can safeguard your mental well-being and lower the risk of burnout linked to excessive technology use by striking a balance between screen time and offline activities.

Determining Limits on Social Media Use

If social media is not used appropriately, it may be a major cause of stress. It's essential to establish limits on your social media use if you want to keep your relationship with technology positive.

- **Set Time Limits for Social Media:** Establish explicit time restrictions for your daily social media usage. To monitor and control your usage, use apps like Digital Wellbeing for Android or Screen Time for iOS.

- **"Culture Your Feed:"** Follow accounts that motivate, enlighten, or encourage you. Mute or unfollow accounts that make you feel anxious or depressed. Instead of making you feel anxious or unhappy, social media should make your life better.
- **Avoid Using Social Media Right Before Bed:** Study demonstrates how using social media right before bed can cause anxiety and interfere with sleep cycles. To improve the quality of your sleep, make it a habit to unplug from all screens at least half an hour before bed.

You may lessen social media's detrimental effects on your mental health and preserve your equilibrium by establishing limits on how much time you spend on it.

Mindfully Using Technology

When utilized carefully, technology can be an effective stress-reduction aid. This entails using technology with intention, making sure that it enhances rather than diminishes your wellbeing.

- **Mindful Consumption:** Choose carefully what you read or watch online. Give positive, instructive, and encouraging content first priority.
- **Practice Digital Mindfulness:** Pay close attention to the present when utilizing applications for work or relaxation. Refrain from multitasking and focus entirely on the current work.
- **Create Rituals Without Technology:** Establish daily routines that help you unplug from screens, such meditation in the morning, walks in the evening, or meals with loved ones without electronics.

Using technology mindfully can improve its ability to manage stress and encourage a healthy connection with digital technologies.

In conclusion, there is a lot of promise in using technology for stress management if done carefully and purposefully. People can lessen the detrimental effects of technology on their mental health while optimizing its positive effects on stress management by implementing stress-relieving apps, controlling digital overload, and developing a positive connection with technology.

CHAPTER 9

Expert Techniques to Avoid Burnout

In today's workplace, burnout which is typified by emotional tiredness, depersonalization, and a diminished sense of personal accomplishment is becoming a more prevalent problem. If not properly handled, the strain to fulfill deadlines, control high expectations, and balance several obligations can result in burnout. This chapter examines professional burnout prevention techniques, emphasizing the development of burnout-resistant work environments, self-advocacy, and identifying when a career transition is required. In order to foster long-term wellbeing and sustainable production, each of these tactics is crucial.

9.1 Workplaces That Prevent Burnout

Qualities of a Positive Workplace Environment

The key to avoiding burnout at work is a positive company culture. It creates an atmosphere where workers are encouraged to perform at their highest level and feel appreciated and supported. Among the essential traits of such a culture are:

- **Free Exchange of Information:** Transparency and open communication foster a culture that makes workers feel appreciated and acknowledged. Clear communication between management and employees lessens emotions of alienation and annoyance. Workers should be able to express their thoughts, worries, and difficulties without worrying about being judged. Town halls, feedback sessions, and routine check-ins are good methods to guarantee continuous communication.

- **Deference to Work-Life Harmony:** Work-life balance is valued in a company that resists burnout. This entails creating an atmosphere where personal time is valued in addition to encouraging workers to take time off. To enable workers to rest, employers should encourage remote work choices, flexible work schedules, and fair vacation policies.

- **Acknowledgment and gratitude:** Maintaining motivation and avoiding burnout requires acknowledging efforts and accomplishments. Emotional weariness is less common among workers who believe their efforts are appreciated and recognized. Public acclaim during meetings, cash bonuses, or modest prizes for reaching milestones are just a few ways that people can show their appreciation.

- **The safety of psychological aspects:** Trust and participation are increased in an environment where workers feel free to voice their thoughts and make errors without worrying about the repercussions. By avoiding the stagnation of both professional and personal development, psychological safety promotes creativity, innovation, and personal growth—all of which contribute to a reduction in burnout.

- A welcoming and encouraging environment Feelings

of alienation can be lessened in an inclusive workplace where diversity is valued and staff members are treated with respect for who they are. In addition to lowering pressures that could lead to burnout, inclusivity promotes a feeling of belonging.

- Establishing a positive workplace culture improves overall organizational performance in addition to the well-being of individuals. A business that places a high priority on the mental and emotional well-being of its workers is more likely to see increased job satisfaction, increased productivity, and decreased turnover rates.

Ways in Which Employers Can Encourage Employee Welfare

In order to promote employee well-being and avoid burnout, employers play a critical role. Employers may have a big impact by putting strategies and policies that promote mental health into practice. Among the crucial steps are:

- **Offering Resources for Mental Health:** Access to mental health services including treatment stipends, Employee Assistance Programs (EAPs), and counseling should be provided by employers. These resources equip workers with the skills they need to deal with stress and ask for assistance when needed.

- **Establishing Reasonable Expectations:** Burnout can occur rapidly as a result of unrealistic task expectations. Employers are responsible for making sure that workers are not asked to take on more work than they can reasonably accomplish and that the burden is manageable. Setting specific, attainable goals and allocating the resources required to achieve them are crucial.

- **Encouraging Time Off and Breaks:** Employers must proactively urge staff members to utilize their vacation days and take frequent breaks throughout the workday. By guaranteeing that workers have time to relax and rejuvenate, this helps avoid burnout. Additionally, businesses might include "mental health days" in their benefits package.

- **Providing Professional Growth:** By giving workers a sense of advancement and accomplishment, encouraging them to develop professionally and learn new skills can help avoid burnout. Employers should encourage the professional and personal growth of their staff members through mentorship programs, online courses, and workshops.

- **Building Team Cohesion:** Employees can navigate stress together and receive emotional support from strong relationships among team members. Companies can help employees develop this by planning team-building exercises, boosting cooperation, and fostering a sense of unity among team members.

Employers must develop an organizational mindset that prioritizes work-life balance and mental wellness in addition to these doable tactics. Setting a good example and encouraging others in the company to put their mental health first are two benefits of leadership that genuinely cares about employee well-being.

9.2 Standing Up for What You Want

Expressing Requirements and Limitations at Work

- To avoid burnout, you must speak out for yourself. Clearly expressing your demands and establishing boundaries with your boss and coworkers is one of the first steps in this process. You can keep control over your task and protect your wellbeing by being able to communicate honestly and assertively.

- **Be Aware of Your Limitations:** Knowing your personal limitations in terms of work capability is crucial. Long-term burnout can be avoided by identifying when you're feeling overburdened and admitting when you need a break or more help. You can speak up for yourself without feeling bad if you know your limits.

- **Use Clear and Direct Communication:** Be assertive, explicit, and clear when establishing boundaries. For instance, be upfront about your difficulties with an overwhelming task and provide a workable solution. Say something like, "I have X amount of tasks that need my attention," rather than, "I'm too busy." Could we delegate some of them to other team members or can we talk about which ones are the most urgent?

- **Establish Limits with Technology:** Work and personal time can easily overlap in today's hyper connected society. Maintaining a healthy work-life balance requires setting clear limits around technology, such as turning off email notifications after hours or setting your work phone to "do not disturb."

- **Acquire the Ability to Say No:** One of the most crucial abilities in self-advocacy is the ability to say "no" when it's necessary. Accepting every request, especially if it goes beyond your comfort zone, causes stress and overcommitment. When you are unable to take on additional work, learn how to politely decline and provide an explanation.

Maintaining a healthy work-life balance at work requires the ability to express your demands and boundaries in an effective manner. It gives you the ability to manage your workload, lower stress levels, and avoid burnout.

Strategies for Handling Workload and Due Dates

Another crucial component of self-advocacy is negotiating workload and deadlines. The following are some tactics for establishing reasonable deadlines and negotiating more manageable workloads:

- **Evaluate Your Priorities:** Prior to negotiating workload, evaluate your current obligations and rank the most critical activities. Recognize which jobs should be assigned to others or rescheduled, and which you can manage yourself. Be specific about which responsibilities you can take on and which ones require reassignment while bargaining.

- **Provide reasonable deadlines:** When assigned an assignment, make sure the due date is reasonable considering your current workload. Don't be afraid to propose a more realistic timeline if it isn't. Provide context for your request: "I would need more time to ensure this task is completed at the quality you expect, given my current workload."

- **Provide Solutions:** Be ready to provide solutions when talking to a supervisor about your workload. This could entail suggesting a temporary reorganization of work, assigning some responsibilities to others, or prioritizing others. You show your dedication to the task at hand and promote your own welfare by offering workable answers.

- **Be Receptive to Input:** Since negotiation is a two-way process, be receptive to criticism and prepared to make concessions when necessary. Have discussions centered on identifying solutions that satisfy your demands and the objectives of your company.

Employees can establish a productive workplace without sacrificing mental health by becoming experts at negotiating workload and deadlines.

9.3 Changing to a Healthier Professional Path

Understanding When a Job Change Is Required

Sometimes an unfavorable work atmosphere or an unsuitable job match make burnout inevitable, even with the best efforts to regulate workload and set boundaries. For long-term wellbeing, knowing when to switch to a healthier job path is essential.

- **Indications of Chronic Burnout:** It could be time to think about a change if you frequently feel exhausted, disinterested, and uninspired at work. Fatigue, irritation, and a lack of fulfillment are examples of persistent burnout symptoms that may be signs that your present position or career path isn't fulfilling you.

- The work environment is unhealthy. Burnout can be greatly exacerbated by a bad workplace culture, ongoing conflict, or a lack of leadership support.

Moving to a healthier setting can be required if these problems are not resolved over time.

- **Insufficient Career Advancement:** Burnout and frustration may result if you believe that your current position is stagnating and that there are no chances for development or promotion. Motivation and job satisfaction may suffer from a lack of fresh challenges or educational chances.

Avoiding long-term detrimental impacts on mental health requires being aware of the symptoms of burnout and recognizing when to make a change.

How to Go After a More Satisfying Career

Making the switch to a healthier job path calls for thoughtful preparation and calculated action. The following actions will help you seek a more satisfying career:

- **Self-Evaluation:** Think about your values, interests, and strong points. What do you like best about your current position? What do you wish to alter? You can find the kind of employment that fits with your beliefs by taking the time to evaluate your goals and passions.

- **Investigate Alternative Career Paths:** Look into exciting employment options that fit your values and skill set. Take into account any further training, education, or qualifications that might facilitate the move. Making connections with experts in the field you want to pursue can yield insightful information.

- **Make Little Moves:** Changing careers doesn't have to happen right away. Begin with modest actions, like looking for part-time work, doing freelance work, or working on side projects. Before making a complete switch, you can test the waters with these small adjustments.

- **Contact Support:** It's crucial to get advice from peers who have had similar adjustments, mentors, or career coaches because professional transitions can be difficult. They can provide guidance, support, and useful pointers for a seamless transfer.

Examples of People Who Changed Their Courses and Overcame Burnout

Changing occupations or industries has helped many people overcome burnout. For instance, a marketing executive who switched to freelancer writing discovered that it gave her the freedom and flexibility she needed to restore her work-life balance. Likewise, a software developer who transitioned to a job in data analysis that offered fresh challenges without the strain of long hours and never-ending deadlines.

People can feel more empowered to make changes that result in healthier, more meaningful jobs by learning from the experiences of others.

In summary, proactive organizational and individual initiatives are necessary to prevent burnout. Employees may preserve their long-term mental and emotional health by fostering work environments that are resistant to burnout, speaking up for their own needs, and understanding when to seek a career change. It is the duty of employers to support their employees by cultivating a work-life balance, health, and well-being culture. By using these expert techniques, people can avoid burnout and succeed in the long run.

CHAPTER 10

Long-Term Methods for Maintaining Health

Long-term well-being is a dynamic process that calls for intentional work, careful planning, and ongoing introspection. Building a foundation for long-term health is essential in a society where stress and burnout are frequently caused by societal expectations, fast technological advancements, and external influences. With an emphasis on developing a sustainable routine, remaining flexible in a constantly shifting environment, and making a commitment to ongoing self-care, this chapter examines important long-term techniques to maintain well-being. Every one of these tactics is essential for fostering mental, emotional, and physical well-being, which in turn leads to a balanced and satisfying existence.

10.1 Establishing a Long-Term Routine

Creating Routines That Support Long-Term Health

- Establishing a sustainable routine is the first step towards long-term well-being. Long-term success depends on routines because they give people discipline, lessen decision fatigue, and help them stay focused. Developing well-being-promoting habits takes time, persistence, and intentionality.

- **Begin Small:** Starting with tiny, doable activities is the key to creating long-lasting habits. Focus on small, gradual gains rather than making big, abrupt changes. For example, if increasing your physical activity is your aim, begin by adding only 10 to 15 minutes of physical activity each day. As the habit solidifies, gradually increase the duration and intensity.

- Consistency is more important than perfection. Consistency, not perfection, is the foundation of habits. It's critical to recognize that obstacles will arise during the journey. It just indicates that you need to get back on track; missing a day or two of a new habit does not indicate failure. In the end, consistency is what turns behaviors into habits that support long-term wellbeing.

- **Make Routines Fun:** Selecting activities that you truly enjoy or find meaningful is essential when forming habits. For instance, instead of making yourself eat things that seem like a job, if your objective is to improve your diet, concentrate on adding nutritious items that you genuinely enjoy. Long-lasting behaviors are more likely to be enjoyable.

- **Employing Habit Stacking:** One strategy is habit stacking, which is combining a new habit with an already-existing one. For example, you can quickly include a new habit, like stretching or meditation, after your morning coffee consumption. By using your existing routines, this approach facilitates the adoption of new ones.

Knowing what works best for you personally is essential to developing habits that support long-term well-being. Create a schedule that promotes mental, emotional, and physical well-being, and make sure that these behaviors become ingrained in your everyday routine.

Rituals' Contribution to Stress Reduction

Rituals are an effective way to lower stress and enhance wellbeing. Rituals are frequently infused with personal significance and intention, whereas habits are activities carried out on a regular basis. They offer emotional support, cultivate mindfulness, and contribute to stability. Stress reduction can be greatly aided by incorporating meaningful routines into your daily schedule.

- **Daily Routines:** A good start to the day can be achieved by establishing a morning routine. A glass of water, deep breathing techniques, journaling, or going for a walk could all be part of a morning routine. By beginning each day with a self-care ritual, you prime your body and mind to meet the challenges that lie ahead.

- **Conscious Pauses:** Rituals don't have to be drawn out or difficult. Burnout can be avoided and stress can be managed with a simple routine, like taking a five-minute break every hour to stretch or engage in deep breathing. These little mindfulness exercises serve as resets, giving you the energy and focus you need to go back to work.

- **Evening Customs:** An evening ritual gets you ready for relaxing and getting a good night's sleep, much like a morning ritual sets the tone for the day. Evening routines could involve reading, taking stock of the day's achievements, being grateful, or doing simple body stretches to unwind. These routines help you sleep better and feel less anxious by telling your brain when it's time to relax.

In a world that is frequently busy, rituals offer times for rest and introspection. They can encourage emotional control, mindfulness, and a feeling of wellbeing when done regularly.

10.2 Maintaining Flexibility in a Changing Environment

Accepting Change Without Adding to Your Stress

Adaptability is crucial for preserving wellbeing in the quickly changing environment of today. Whether it is due to changes in one's personal situation, career, or general cultural tendencies, change is unavoidable. But accepting change without giving in to stress calls for a proactive attitude and coping mechanisms for ambiguity.

- **Change Your Viewpoint:** Try to reframe change as a chance for personal development rather than as a danger. You can approach change with interest rather than fear if you see it as a positive thing. Ask yourself, "What can I learn from this?" whenever you encounter change. or "How can this make things better for me?"

- **Establish Resilience**: The capacity to overcome hardship is resilience. The secret to handling the stress that comes with change is to build resilience. Developing emotional fortitude, remaining in touch with a support system, and preserving a sense of direction are all components of resilience building.

People who are resilient are more inclined to view obstacles as short-term and manageable rather than long-term and overpowering.

- **Pay Attention to What You Can Control:** A sense of unpredictability is frequently brought on by change. Instead of focusing on things that are beyond your control, try to manage your stress by concentrating on the elements of the situation that you can influence. For instance, you might not be able to control the change in duties if your job changes, but you can manage how you react to such changes by learning new skills, getting clarity, or changing your perspective.

- **Exercise Adaptability:** Being adaptable is a crucial quality while dealing with change. It entails having an open mind to new ideas and being prepared to modify your goals and expectations. Flexibility training helps you develop an adaptive mentality that makes you more capable of managing unforeseen circumstances.

It takes both a mental shift and the acquisition of coping mechanisms to adjust to change without making things more stressful. You can deal with life's uncertainties more easily if you accept change as a chance for personal development and concentrate on the things you can control.

Increasing Your Mental and Emotional Adaptability

To maintain long-term well-being, mental and emotional flexibility are essential. Challenges are a normal aspect of the human experience, and life is unpredictable. The more adaptable your thoughts and emotions are, the more resilient and well-rounded you will be.

- **Adaptability of the Mind:** Cognitive flexibility is the capacity to change viewpoints and modify your way of thinking in response to novel facts or difficulties. Rather than becoming inflexible or trapped in a certain style of thinking, this mental flexibility enables you to modify your tactics and choices as necessary. Reframing negative beliefs, questioning your presumptions, and remaining receptive to new ideas are all components of cognitive flexibility.

- **Emotional Adaptability:** The capacity to control and modify your emotional reactions according to the circumstances is known as emotional flexibility. Emotionally flexible people are able to evaluate the situation and respond in a balanced manner rather than acting rashly or rigidly. By engaging in mindfulness exercises, learning to identify and categorize your feelings, and applying emotional regulation strategies like cognitive reframing or deep breathing, you can cultivate emotional flexibility.

- **Keeping Stability and Adaptability in Check:** It's crucial to be adaptable, but it's equally critical to preserve stability. Finding the fundamental beliefs or ideals that direct your choices is necessary to strike a balance between the desire for stability and the capacity for adaptation. You may maintain your adaptability without losing sight of your priorities by firmly establishing these principles in your mind.

Gaining mental and emotional flexibility enables you to

remain composed and balanced when faced with uncertainty. It helps you to react to life's changes with fortitude instead of becoming overpowered or inflexible.

10.3 An Unwavering Dedication to Self-Care

Prioritizing Self-Care Above All Elements

An essential component of long-term wellbeing is self-care. It entails making conscious efforts to look after your mental, emotional, and physical well-being. Maintaining resilience, energy, and attention over time requires making self-care a top priority.

- **Make self-care a regular priority:** Self-care should be viewed as a continuous practice, even if many people only treat themselves occasionally. Whether it's exercising, spending time with loved ones, or doing things that make you happy, include self-care activities into your daily schedule. Regularly putting self-care first promotes emotional resilience and helps avoid burnout.

- **Customize Your Self-Care Practice:** There is no one-size-fits-all method of self-care. Customizing your regimen according to what suits you best is crucial. While reading may help some people relax, hiking and other outdoor pursuits may be more appealing to others. Find the self-care practices that benefit your body and mind, then include them into your daily schedule.

- **Establish Limits to Safeguard Your Time:** Setting boundaries that safeguard your time is essential if you want to make self-care a top priority. This entails learning to decline obligations that deplete your energy and giving priority to pursuits that promote your wellbeing. You can make sure you have the mental and physical room to take care of yourself by managing your time well.

Reviewing and Modifying Stress Reduction Techniques as Necessary

The techniques that you find effective at one stage of your life may need to be modified as your situation evolves because stress management is a continuous process. It's critical to periodically review and evaluate your stress-reduction techniques.

- **Consistent Introspection:** Regularly take some time to consider your stress levels and coping mechanisms. Are your present strategies still working? Do you need to deal with any new stressors? You might find areas that require improvement by examining your stress management strategy on a regular basis.

- **Adjusting to Changes in Life:** Your stress management strategies may need to change as your life progresses, whether it's due to increased obligations, work changes, or personal milestones. Adopt a flexible mindset and be prepared to modify your plan of action in response to changing conditions.

Highlighting Minor Gains to Stay Motivated

Maintaining motivation and cultivating a sense of success

requires acknowledging and applauding minor accomplishments. Every action you do to enhance your wellbeing is a triumph worth celebrating. You may maintain motivation on your path to long-term well-being and promote beneficial behaviors by acknowledging and applauding these accomplishments, no matter how minor.

- **Recognize Your Progress:** Spend some time recognizing your accomplishments, whether they include forming a new habit or effectively managing tension in a difficult circumstance. Acknowledging these minor victories strengthens your resolve to maintain your long-term health and helps you gain momentum.

- **Give yourself a reward:** Giving yourself a reward for minor accomplishments strengthens the link between effort and reward and offers positive reinforcement. Rewarding yourself with a soothing pastime or just pausing to consider your accomplishments will help you stay motivated and boost your self-esteem.

To sum up, sustained well-being necessitates a dedication to self-care, flexibility, and sustainable routines. People can lay a solid foundation for long-lasting mental and emotional well-being by developing healthy habits and rituals, accepting change with grace, and acknowledging their accomplishments. These techniques enable people to successfully negotiate life's obstacles while preserving their equilibrium and prospering in a world that is constantly changing.

ABOUT THE AUTHOR

Harmony Royce is a dedicated healthcare worker who has a strong interest in holistic wellness. Harmony's extensive history in various aspects of health and wellness provides her with a wealth of knowledge and expertise that she can utilize in her writing and professional endeavors.

Harmony is a talented author who crafts thought-provoking books that inspire readers to have well-rounded, balanced lives. She writes about a variety of health-related topics, such as diet, exercise, mental health, and mindfulness. Her approachable writing style combines practical guidance with evidence-based research to make complex health concepts approachable and engaging for readers of all ages.

Harmony actively promotes the benefits of holistic health through writing, community workshops, and internet forums. Her mission is to educate and inspire people about the transformative power of self-care and healthy lifestyle choices.

www.ingramcontent.com/pod-product-compliance
Lightning Source LLC
Chambersburg PA
CBHW071033240526
45469CB00006BD/2192